Sandcastles on the Beach

A Play

John McColl

A Samuel French Acting Edition

SAMUELFRENCH-LONDON.CO.UK
SAMUELFRENCH.COM

Copyright © 1990 by Samuel French Ltd
All Rights Reserved

SANDCASTLES ON THE BEACH is fully protected under the copyright laws of the British Commonwealth, including Canada, the United States of America, and all other countries of the Copyright Union. All rights, including professional and amateur stage productions, recitation, lecturing, public reading, motion picture, radio broadcasting, television and the rights of translation into foreign languages are strictly reserved.

ISBN 978-0-573-12237-8

www.samuelfrench-london.co.uk

www.samuelfrench.com

FOR AMATEUR PRODUCTION ENQUIRIES

UNITED KINGDOM AND WORLD EXCLUDING NORTH AMERICA
plays@SamuelFrench-London.co.uk
020 7255 4302/01

Each title is subject to availability from Samuel French,
depending upon country of performance.

CAUTION: Professional and amateur producers are hereby warned that *SANDCASTLES ON THE BEACH* is subject to a licensing fee. Publication of this play does not imply availability for performance. Both amateurs and professionals considering a production are strongly advised to apply to the appropriate agent before starting rehearsals, advertising, or booking a theatre. A licensing fee must be paid whether the title is presented for charity or gain and whether or not admission is charged.

The professional rights in this play are controlled by Samuel French Ltd, 52 Fitzroy Street, London, W1T 5JR.

No one shall make any changes in this title for the purpose of production. No part of this book may be reproduced, stored in a retrieval system, or transmitted in any form, by any means, now known or yet to be invented, including mechanical, electronic, photocopying, recording, videotaping, or otherwise, without the prior written permission of the publisher. No one shall upload this title, or part of this title, to any social media websites.

The right of John McColl to be identified as author of this work has been asserted by him in accordance with Section 77 of the Copyright, Designs and Patents Act 1988

SANDCASTLES ON THE BEACH

The play was first performed in May 1988 at the Netherbow Arts Centre by the Canongate Theatre Company with the following cast:

Marge	Mary Christie
Butter, her husband	John Cole
Weston, her son	Jon O'Kane
Trish, their daughter-in-law	Helen Aitken
Director	Helen Aitken

The action of the play takes place in the old-fashioned living-room of Marge and Butter

Time—present

For Helen
With love and thanks

SANDCASTLES ON THE BEACH

The sitting-room of Marge and Butter. It is evening

The room is very old-fashioned. Indeed, little has changed in the room during the couple's fifty-three year stay. There are two exits, the first leads to the hall and the second to the kitchen. The furniture consists of a bookcase, a coffee-table and seating for four people, which includes a settee

As the CURTAIN *rises, Marge, an elderly woman, is standing by the window and Butter, her husband, is sitting by the coal fire*

There is a pause

Marge That's another day, then.

There is silence

Butter Bin day tomorrow.
Marge (*turning*) No.
Butter Wednesday.
Marge Oh Lord, there's always something, isn't there? Always something that wants doing, that wants worrying about.
Butter Nothing to worry about putting the bins out, Marge. I'll do it later.
Marge (*sharply*) No. I'm not having you lifting, Dad. Weston'll do it. We'll ask him when he comes. Put it down on the things-to-do pad.
Butter Right-o. (*He writes*)

There is a pause

Marge I'm glad you asked him to come.
Butter We've got to tell him, haven't we?
Marge But I'm glad you asked him to come. Not told him over the phone. I'm glad.
Butter It's not really the sort of thing you can say on the phone, is it?

There is a pause

Marge We've not seen him for such a long time. Such a long time.
Butter Three months, Marge. That's all.
Marge (*again sharply*) That's a long time. Just you remember that. That's a long time, still. (*Pause*) Red sky at night ...
Butter Sailor's delight. (*Pause*) He said he had some news for us as well.
Marge What sort of news?
Butter He wouldn't say. Good news, though, he said that much. He'll tell us when he gets here.

There is a pause

Marge What day's today?
Butter Tuesday.
Marge No, Dad, I know it's Tuesday. *EastEnders* was on, course it's Tuesday. What date is it?
Butter The first of September.

There is a slight pause

Marge I know that, too.
Butter Then why the dickens are you asking?
Marge I wanted to know if you knew. If you remembered. Do you?
Butter I've just told you, Marge.
Marge You don't, do you?
Butter The first of September ...
Marge Our first date. Fifty-five years ago today. The first of September.
Butter (*remembering fondly*) High tea with your mother ...
Marge Buttered scones and jam ...
Butter And twenty questions to follow. Scared me rigid, your old mum.
Marge You had to be on your best behaviour then.
Butter My very best. Didn't want to slip up with your old mum. (*Pause*) I fancied you rotten, Marge, and that's the truth of it. Prettiest waitress in Lyon's coffee house.
Marge One lump or two ...?
Butter (*laughing*) That's how it started. One lump or two ...
Marge And you were drinking cola. I thought it was black coffee.
Butter No, you didn't. You were trying to make conversation. I understood. I got the message.

Marge You were too shy to say anything yourself.
Butter One lump or two and, pow! Fifty-three years of married life. We haven't done too badly, have we?
Marge No. We've done all right, you and I. We've done all right.

There is a pause

Butter Prettiest waitress in Lyon's coffee house, that's what you were. You could give them a run for their money now.
Marge (*giggling*) Oh you ... (*Pause*) We had some great times, though, didn't we? Cinemas, picnics, walks—my Lord, the walks we used to have. Miles and miles we'd go. Hill walks and nature rambles from dawn 'til dusk.
Butter Your poor old mum. Don't know what she thought we got up to.
Marge I've a pretty good idea. We can't blame her, either. I'd come home looking like I'd been dragged backwards through a hedge.
Butter She needn't have worried. You had been dragged backwards through a hedge!

They laugh

Ay, Marge. That was another day. We can't complain, can we?
Marge Until now.
Butter Even now, Marge. Even now.

There is a pause

Marge (*turning back to the window*) I wish Weston would come. Where is he? Weston'll make me laugh. He'll pick me up and he'll tickle me and I'll just have to laugh and laugh. And I won't stop laughing until—until we have to tell him.
Butter And tell him what we've decided to do.

There is a slight pause

Marge I don't think I'll tell him that.
Butter You must.
Marge Not tonight. He'll bring her with him. I don't want to tell him in front of her.
Butter Oh Marge, Trish is family. She has to know.
Marge No she's not. Not real family.

Butter You're just being daft. Course she's family. Weston's wife...
Marge And don't we all know why she married him? To muscle in on his business, that's why.
Butter Why do you say things like that? Weston doesn't say that.
Marge Mrs Rose...
Butter (*disparagingly*) Mrs Rose.
Marge Read an article about Miss Patricia the other day. In that fashion magazine. (*Pronouncing it Vo-gu*) Vogue. She gave it me. (*She goes to the bookcase and looks for the cutting*)
Butter I never realized she was famous. No wonder so many people turned up at the church. There must have been about two hundred on her side. There was only twenty on ours.
Marge There was more than twenty.
Butter Not much more.
Marge (*finding the article*) Here it is.
Butter Read it out, then.
Marge (*reading*) "Top model, twenty-four-year-old Patricia Kennedy, who last year became one of Britain's most sought-after fashion models, has married provincial modelling agent Winston Mair"—here, they've spelt his name wrong.
Butter That'll be the typesetters, love. Ignorant lot.
Marge (*reading again*) "Has married provincial modelling agent Weston Mair in London. Immediately after the wedding, Patricia announced that she was giving up modelling to become a partner in Wilson's agency." They've done it again, Dad. That's two different names they've given him and neither of them right. (*Pause. Reading*) "Said Miss Kennedy: 'Life at the top in this profession is short and hard. I've no regrets about leaving it behind!' Well, Patricia, as the cliché goes, it must be love—or something. Watch this space!" That's it. There she is in the photograph. Dolled up to the nines. And there's Weston's shoulder.
Butter Top model, eh? She must have been on an earner. What's so bad about that?
Marge Mrs Rose says it's what they call an insinuating article. "It must be love—or something." Mrs Rose says they don't think it's love at all. They think she married Weston because she knows her career can't last forever. She's after security, that's all.

Butter Sounds to me like they think she's daft throwing it all away to marry Weston.
Marge Well, Mrs Rose says ...
Butter Anyway, what does it matter what Mrs Rose says, or Vogu, or anyone else? She's our daughter-in-law and I'm proud of her.
Marge You haven't met her, hardly.
Butter Well, I'm proud of her. Sounds like she's sacrificed a lot to marry our son.
Marge It's all a matter of opinion, Dad, and I'm afraid I've got mine. (*Pause*) I'm sorry, we shouldn't be fighting like this.
Butter We're not fighting, Marge. Good healthy argument, that's what this is. We've had plenty of those.
Marge It's just that we never see Weston any more. Not since they were wed and that was in June. He used to be here all the time. He just phones on Sundays now. She's come between the three of us.
Butter He'll be here tonight. That's what counts. And you'll get a chance to know Trish. I think you'll like her.

There is silence

Marge moves to the window

Marge There's no sign of them.
Butter It's a good drive from the city. Give them a chance.
Marge It's a quarter past eight, turned.
Butter He'll be working late, likely. Agents can't just pick and choose their hours, you know. They have to work late, sometimes.

There is a pause

Marge What's on the telly?
Butter I've looked. Pop programmes. Nothing on 'til the news.
Marge We can do without pop programmes. We'll catch the news at nine. (*Pause*) We had to make do without the telly before. We had to make our own entertainment.
Butter We managed all right.
Marge Never a dull moment. Come rain or shine, there was always something. Always something ...

There is a pause

Butter Perhaps if . . .
Marge If?
Butter If we'd made friends more, socialized . . .
Marge I only ever wanted you, Dad.
Butter And I burned for you, my love. My heart would leap ten feet in the air whenever you walked into the room. And it still does. Even after all these years, I can honestly say that it still does. (*Pause*) But if we'd gone with people more, socialized, you wouldn't be on your own . . .
Marge But I won't be on my own. I'll still have you. I'll still have you, don't you see? That's why. That's why . . . (*Pause*) How're you feeling?
Butter I'm all right.
Marge Sickly feeling gone?
Butter Damn radium. I'm glad I'm off that. Makes you sick as a dog. (*Pause*) None of that now. (*Pause*) Marge . . .
Marge I remember the very first time I ever saw you being sick. You'd had a bellyful that night. Three weeks married, we were. Three weeks. It was all over the bedclothes and down your honeymoon pyjamas. Those stripey ones you never wear now . . .
Butter (*earnestly*) Marge . . .
Marge No. I won't talk about it anymore. No. My mind is made up.
Butter Weston won't like it. He won't understand it.
Marge He'll just have to like it. It's what I want. (*Pause*) You understand, don't you?
Butter Course I do. I know why.

They hold hands

Marge Oh where is he? It's dark now and we've not been for our walk.
Butter Cancer. Tame sort of a word, isn't it. (*Pause*) I remember when they first told me. Dr Phillips—poor little bugger. He said, Butter, he said, in you come, have a seat. Just like he was asking me in for a drink and a chat. (*Laughs*) Fancy that, eh. Me, being asked in for a drink and a chat by doctor types. (*Laughs*) All right, I said. All right, I'll have a pint of bitter. That's what I said. He laughed. And when he stopped laughing, he told me, "You've got cancer." Just like that. Blurted it out. Didn't know how to tell me, see. He was young. (*Pause*) I just sat there for a

moment and said nothing. He must have thought I was taking some sort of a turn, because he was up out of his seat and running like Eric Liddle to fetch me a glass of water. But I wasn't taking any turn. I was just thinking, what a tame sort of a word. Like mumps. Chickenpox sounds ten times worse to me. (*Pause*) "We'll fight it, Butter," he said, "We'll fight it and we'll beat it, I promise you that." He shouldn't have made promises. He was young. It would have been a real let-down if I'd believed him. I knew. I knew I had it and I knew I'd keep it. He couldn't look me in the eye on Friday. He kept saying how he couldn't understand how it had got this far. And I swear—I swear I saw a tear in his eye. Unprofessional. "I'm sorry," he said. Why? What's he sorry for? God Almighty, I've had more years than most. I'll probably have more than him when all's said and done. I reckon he's got high blood pressure. (*Pause*) What was it the *Daily Mirror* said today? Kiddie killed himself sniffing glue. That's who I feel sorry for. Him and others like him. They never had a chance. Never had a chance to experience what we had. Fifty-three years and he's sorry for me! Fifty-three years we've been married and at the end of it all, we've got the chance to say goodbye properly and with dignity. What more could a man ask for?

Marge holds Butter tightly

Marge I love you.

A car horn is heard

He's here. (*She rushes to the window*) He's seen me. He's waving (*Calling*) Oo-oo, Weston! Oo-oo! Oh, and there's Patricia. Dolled up to the nines.
Butter I'll get the door.
Marge Stay where you are. (*She goes to the door*) Oh Dad, I'm shaking. Look at my hands, they're shaking.

The doorbell rings frantically

How am I going to tell him?
Butter We, Marge. We're going to tell him. Together. (*Pause*) Go on, then, let the lad in. (*Short pause*) Go on, we've waited long enough to see him.

Marge exits

Butter closes the curtains and switches on a lamp. Voices are heard in the hall

Weston (*off*) Where is he? Where is he?

Weston enters. He is in his forties, chubby and balding

Trish follows him. She is an attractive, but not beautiful, twenty-four year old. She is not made-up extravagantly and she is not over-dressed. She is quite obviously pregnant

Marge also enters

Weston (*moving straight to Butter*) Butter! (*He hugs his father*) You look marvellous! Marge, isn't he a picture?
Butter I feel fine, son.
Weston Do you? Do you really?
Butter Course.
Weston What about the pains? They gone?
Butter They've given me these tablets, son ...
Weston (*sharply*) Pills?
Marge In you come, Patricia.
Weston Yes, come on Trish, stop skulking at the back there. Sit down on the settee. And you sit beside her, Marge, and let me take a look at you.
Marge No, no, no, not me. I've got to put the kettle on ...
Weston Never you mind the kettle, I'll see to the bloody kettle. You just park your bum beside my missus and do as you're told.
Marge (*laughing and sitting*) You haven't changed. (*To Trish*) He hasn't changed.
Weston You look as beautiful as ever, my old darling. Still the prettiest waitress, eh Butter?
Butter That's right, son.
Weston And what about Trish, eh? Take a look at my missus over there.
Marge Very nice, Patricia. Nice dress.
Trish Thank you.
Weston Put on a bit of weight since you last saw her, don't you think?
Trish (*smiling*) Weston ...
Marge Well, what with you retiring, I suppose you're not as active as you were.
Weston Oh, I keep her busy enough in the office, Marge, don't

you worry about that. Not that she'll be in the office for much longer.

Marge Giving that up too, are you?

Weston Well, she's going to have to, Marge. (*To Trish*) Shall I tell them now?

Trish Why not get the tea first?

Butter Tell us what?

Weston The news, Butter. The earth-shattering, front page news I've got for you. But it's going to have to wait until after tea and scones. I take it, it is tea and scones on the menu tonight?

Marge He knows. It's always tea and scones when we have visitors.

Weston He knows, you knows! Tea and scones for four coming right up.

Marge The scones are in the oven. Give them a heat.

Trish (*getting up*) I'll give you a hand.

Weston Sit! You just stay where you are. Sit!

Marge (*joining in the Barbara Woodhouse impersonation*) Sit! Sit!

Trish, embarrassed, sits

Weston exits

Trish You'd think he was at home the way he carries on.

Marge Well, he is at home. His proper home. He was brought up in this house, you know.

Weston (*poking his head round the door*) And, if you're very lucky, there might be something a little stronger than tea to wash down the scones.

Weston exits

Marge What could he have meant by that?

Butter He'll have brought a bottle with him. That right, Trish?

Trish (*smiling*) That's right.

Marge That's just like him. Always thinking about something like that. Always thinking about his mum and dad. We're lucky, aren't we, Dad? To have a son like Weston. He cares for his parents. Not like some.

Butter He's always getting us little presents, buying us this and that.

Marge (*suddenly sharp*) But presents aren't everything. Any son can get presents. Weston can afford it. He's done well for

himself, I'm sure you know that only too well, Patricia. There are other ways of showing that you care for your mum and dad. Like visiting . . .
Butter Like he's doing tonight.
Marge Yes. (*Pause*) Do you know, Patricia, that in Japan, they don't have old age pensions. No, it's the custom over there for the children to look after their parents when they're old. That's their responsibility. And that's more important than having pennies in your pocket that can't hardly buy you anything anymore. Don't you agree?
Trish Yes, I . . . yes.
Butter (*hurriedly*) What's he brought for us this time, Trish?
Trish What?
Butter Weston. What's he brought for us?
Trish Champagne.

There is a pause

Marge Oh.
Trish He just thought that, since we've all got some good news . . .
Butter He's jumped to conclusions . . .
Marge We should have told him on the phone, Dad . . .
Butter Just makes things a little harder, that's all. No harm done.

There is silence

Marge You've never seen this house, have you, Patricia? Weston grew up here, spent his happiest years, I like to think.
Trish I was here just before the wedding.
Butter You're not thinking right, Marge, you remember when Trish was here.
Marge Oh stupid, stupid, stupid! My memory . . .
Butter Not what it used to be.
Trish It was five months ago.
Marge Yes. A long time.

There is a pause

Butter You look different, Trish. Mind you, the last time we saw you, you was all in white. My, that was a day to remember.
Marge It was more off-white as I remember, Dad. Cream. (*To Trish*) You'll have the photographs.

Trish (*apologetically*) I have, but I haven't. I'm sorry. It was such a rush to get here. I completely forgot.
Marge Oh.
Butter Never mind. We'll see them some other time.

There is silence

Marge How's Weston's business?
Trish Fine. (*Pause*) Well, struggling, really. Seems to be nothing but bills at the moment.
Butter You choose the girls now, do you? Now that you're retired from active service, as it were?
Marge Retired! That makes her sound like us, doesn't it, Dad?
Trish I keep the books at the moment. It's a full time job, I can tell you. Weston is more involved with the actual clients themselves.
Butter Still got plenty?
Trish Not bad.
Marge Still models, mostly?
Trish Mostly.
Marge He always had an eye for a pretty girl.
Butter Not that he ...
Marge He was always chatting them up, fancying anything in a skirt. He goes through phases. Do you remember, Dad, back in the early days ...
Butter I don't think Trish is interested, Marge ...
Marge He was a card. Still is. Don't know where he gets his energy from.
Butter He's settled down now, though.
Marge He's done well for himself.
Butter He's got Trish.
Marge The business is thriving.

There is a pause

Butter I never understood why he changed his name.
Marge Oh Dad, all theatrical people do that. Weston Mair is much more catchy than Weston Duncock.
Trish He calls himself Super Mair now.
Butter Why?
Marge It's a play on words. (*She giggles*) Weston Super Mair! That's just like him. (*She giggles again*) Where could he have got to with that supper?

Butter Give him a chance, love.
Marge (*getting up*) I'll give him the hurry up, that's what I'll give him. Patricia must be starving after that long drive. It's the first time she's done it, after all.

Marge exits

Trish No, honestly ... I'm all right, honestly ...
Butter No use trying to stop her, love. Once she gets an idea into her head, nothing in the world'll shift it.
Trish I don't think she likes me particularly.
Butter 'Course she does. It's just her way. The three of us are very close, Trish. Sometimes it's hard for someone else to fit into that kind of set-up, that's all.
Trish She adores Weston, doesn't she?
Butter And he adores Marge, and a little bit more still. It's always extremes with those two.
Trish Has he always called you Butter?
Butter Always. It was a mickey take, really. Marge and I have always been close, but, well she couldn't have kids. So we adopted Weston when he was nine. I expect he's told you all that. ... Well, a bit like you, I suppose, he found it wasn't all that easy to fit into a close relationship. It took time for everyone and being a child, he resented that. He was always saying how he couldn't tell us apart. Like Marge and Butter. It just stuck.
Marge Makes you sound like a grocery list.
Butter We gave him a good home. He was happy here. We all were. Even when he moved to the city, he would phone, come home at weekends, that sort of thing. Since you got wed ...
Trish We haven't visited once.
Butter But you're young, trying to settle down, make a new home for yourselves. I understand that. So does Marge, really.
Trish She must think I'm a real homebreaker.
Butter It's difficult for her, Trish. Especially now.

There is a pause

Trish What did you mean just then? That Weston had jumped to conclusions? It's not good news, is it.
Butter No, Trish. Not very.
Trish You're going to die. (*Pause*) How strange. I always thought

you could sense impending doom immediately. There's no sense of it from you or Marge. Weston hasn't got a clue. Neither had I. It's eerie.

Before Butter can reply, Marge is heard screeching in the hall

Weston enters, carrying Marge, who is carrying the tea tray

Marge (*screeching*) I'll drop it! I'll drop it!
Weston One step, two step, tickle you under there!
Trish Weston, for God's sake ...
Butter It's all right, Trish, she won't drop it. They used to do this all the time. Mad, that's what they are.

Marge finally puts the tray down and collapses in a heap on the settee, giggling uncontrollably

There is a pause

Marge We had your Patricia worried there, Weston. Thought we'd spill the tea all down her nice new frock. We've been playing that game too long for that. Since before she was born, I don't doubt.
Weston You're more tickly than you were the last time I was here. What have you been doing to her, Butter. Well, tuck in, Trish doll, tuck in. Marge's best, these are.
Marge Good home cooking. None of your supermarket rubbish.
Weston Prepared by your own fair hand.
Marge I suppose you have to rely on the supermarket, mostly, what with you working?
Trish I manage a little cooking.
Weston And Earl Grey tea. Nothing but the best here. I'll tell you what this is. This is celebration food. So. Let's have some celebration talk, eh?
Marge Weston ...
Weston Sorry, Marge, visitors first. We would like to announce, Trish and I, that on tenth of February, or thereabouts, you will be the proud possessors of a grandson. Or, if something has gone wrong with the plan, a granddaughter. Whatever it is, it's on the way!

There is a pause

Marge Oh.

Weston (*sarcastically*) But, then again, there's a few million kids born every day, so why get excited about this one? Come on, loves, I'm going to be a father!
Butter That is wonderful, Weston. I'm so pleased. (*He moves to Trish*) You must be so happy, Trish. Congratulations.
Weston Come on, Marge. I know what you're thinking. It won't be nine months after the wedding. Well, modern days, love, and this is a modern child. The main thing is that it's going to be healthy. And do you know what we're going to call our bouncing baby boy?
Trish If it is a boy.
Weston Bernard. After you, Dad.
Butter You haven't called me Bernard in your life.
Weston Well, I could hardly go up to the vicar and say I wanted him christened Butter Mair, now could I.
Marge (*hugging him*) Congratulations, love.
Weston That's better.
Butter Why don't we crack open the champagne!
Weston In a minute. Let's hear your news first.
Marge No, Weston, not now.
Weston Come on, Marge.
Trish Later, Weston. We'll talk about it later.
Weston I've only got one bottle of champagne.
Trish Weston, no . . .
Weston What's the big secret? Come on, I want to know.

There is a pause

Marge It's about your dad, Weston.
Weston I had an inkling.
Marge We went in for a check on Friday.
Weston Routine check, that's right. (*Pause*) Well?
Marge He's been taken off the radium.
Weston That is marvellous news, that is absolutely bloody marvellous news! Trish, champagne, get the bloody champagne!
Marge He's been taken off the radium because there's no point in his having it any more.
Weston (*first doubts*) Because, it's gone . . . (*Short pause*) That's right, isn't it? The cancer's gone . . .?
Marge The cancer's spread, Weston. It's spread from his liver and now it's everywhere.

Weston Oh my God ...
Marge They've taken him off the radium because there's no point putting him through the distress.
Weston Dad ... Oh God, Dad ...
Butter They've given me painkillers, son. There's no pain.
Trish (*quietly*) How long?
Butter About three months, they said. At the outside. Probably less.
Weston (*breaking down. Crossing to Butter*) Oh Dad, my Dad, my Dad ...
Butter Weston, Weston this isn't the way, son, this isn't what we want. No tears, none of that stuff. We've got all this time to say goodbye, make arrangements. It's a blessing, son, a blessing.
Weston We can still fight it. (*Breaking from Butter*) We can still beat it.
Butter No ...
Weston They said it would be all right. How could this happen? Listen, I'll get the best for you, Butter. Top specialists, I've got the cash.
Butter No amount of cash is going to stop what I've got growing inside me. We've got to be practical now.

There is a short pause

Weston You're right. You're right, we've got to act normally, sensibly, keep control. Trish. Get the champagne.
Trish We don't need the champagne, Weston.
Weston Get the champagne, Trish, we can still celebrate.

Trish looks to Butter, who nods. Trish exits to fetch the bottle

We can still celebrate. I'm going to be a dad, you're going to be a ... (*He tails off*) Christ, I'm seeing my old mum and dad for the first time in three months. That's cause enough for celebration.
Butter That's it, son.

Trish returns with the bottle

Weston And glasses, Trish, come on.
Butter Kitchen cabinet.

Trish exits

There is a long pause

Weston Well. Look at me. The married man. Didn't think I'd do it, did you?
Butter It's good to see you.
Marge It's good to see you at last.

Trish enters with the glasses

There is a long silence as Weston opens the bottle and pours the champagne

Weston Well. Cheers.

They drink

There is silence

Butter There's something else we wanted to talk to you about.
Weston Anything, Butter. You know that.
Butter The funeral arrangements.

There is a slight pause

Weston Of course. Anything you want. We've got the cash, haven't we? We've had a good spell, lately. Flowing in. Whatever you want, Butter, love. Marble ... whatever ... you know, gravestone ... oh God ... whatever, you choose.
Butter It's not so much that we wanted to discuss.
Weston You haven't been going to church regular, have you? No problems. I'll fix you up. I'm owed a few favours in that line, as a matter of fact. So don't you go worrying on that score. Just leave all the arrangements to me.
Butter No, it's ... (*With great difficulty*) We want to tell you what we've decided to do.
Weston Whatever you like. But remember, both of you, funeral costs, all that, my worry.
Butter There isn't going to be a funeral, Weston.
Weston No funeral?
Marge We're going to have your dad stuffed, love.

There is a slight pause

Butter looks nervously towards Weston

Weston But—but where?
Marge (*slightly surprised by the question*) Well, all over.

Trish chokes on her champagne. Weston looks horrified

Well, then. What do you think?
Butter (*cautiously*) It's only an idea at this stage, son.
Marge But it's what we're going to do. We've decided. We've been to MFI and we've got a nice eight by six glass cabinet ordered. It's got mahogany panelling. Cost a fortune. We're not going to change our minds now.
Weston But Marge . . .
Marge My mind is made up. If you'd been here to discuss it, you'd have understood. But you weren't here. You're never here.
Trish Could I have a glass of water, please.
Butter Of course you can, love.
Marge I'll fetch it, Dad.
Butter Tell you what, why don't I come with you. Get another pot of tea on. Let Weston and Trish . . . ah . . . just let Weston and Trish, eh?

Butter and Marge exit hurriedly

There is a pause

Trish She doesn't mean it, Weston. Not really. It's just shock. Makes you think irrationally.
Weston 'Course she means it, Trish, of course she bloody means it.
Trish Now she does. But in a couple of days' time, when she's had a chance to think, she'll realize she can't possibly.
Weston You don't know Marge. She's stubborn, always has been. Once she gets an idea into her head, that's it. Irrevocable. (*He picks up the notepad by the phone*) It's all down here in the things-to-do-pad: 'Look up taxidermists in the Yellow Pages.' Well, I'm not letting this happen. Christ Almighty, what a mess, eh? What a bloody mess.
Trish Look, love, no-one is going to let this happen. It just can't happen. And she'll see that herself.
Weston Don't be soft, doll. She's even got the display cabinet ordered. All we need now is a large jar of pickles and everything's hunky-dory.
Trish We'll talk to them when they get back.
Weston Talking's no good, Trish. Not with Marge. Action. That's what's needed here, not talk. We've got to get a doctor to her, get her certified, get her locked up, anything, if it stops her from

shoving plaster of Paris up my dad. (*He sits with his head in his hands*)

Trish She must be very unhappy.

Weston She must be off her crust.

Trish It's just reaction, Weston. Reaction to the worst news she's ever had in her life.

Weston Tears. That's what I call reaction. Like the ones I spilled tonight when I heard. I don't mind admitting it, because that is reaction. Human reaction. Seeking the advice of a taxidermist is something altogether more detached.

Trish We all have different ways of expressing grief.

Weston Yes, well, I've got a bit of expressing to do with those two when they get back.

Trish Then I think I'll go for a walk.

Weston Trish . . .

Trish No, it's best that you discuss this between the three of you. I don't think you'll get much out of your mother when I'm around.

Weston Perhaps not. (*He crosses to Trish and holds her*) She likes you, Trish. Honest. Deep down.

Trish Just speak to them. Don't lose your temper, try to understand. Whatever is going on in their minds, try to understand.

They kiss

Trish exits

Marge enters

Marge Where's she going? She's not had her water. What's wrong?

Weston Well, she's just had a bit of a shock, Marge. We both have. You see, I've just been told that I'm going to lose my dad. And then, almost with the same breath, I'm told that he's going on display. That's enough to shock anyone, I fancy.

Butter enters

Butter Where's Trish gone?

Weston For a walk. She won't be long.

Butter Oh.

Weston They won't let you, you know.

Marge I don't know about that. I don't know that it's got anything to do with anyone except me and your dad.
Weston It's against the law, Marge.
Marge There's no law that says you can't have your husband stuffed.
Butter Once he's dead.
Marge That's right.
Weston Not in so many words, no, but . . .
Butter We're taking advice on it, son.
Marge Legal advice.
Weston It's medical advice you want, Marge . . .
Butter Now, don't joke like that, son.
Weston I'm sorry, Butter, I'm not joking. I mean, there has to be something wrong here. What kind of a wife wants to see her husband hanging up on the mantelpiece for years after he's dead?
Marge He won't be on the mantelpiece.
Weston I'm sorry, I forgot. You're getting a glass cabinet.
Butter Mahogany and glass.
Weston I stand corrected. So. Where are you going to put him?
Marge I'm going to clear out your room.
Weston It's a Freudian nightmare!
Marge You never use it any more. I'll never use it for anything, except maybe as a spare bedroom if you ever get round to visiting again.
Weston Hasn't it occurred to you—either of you—that I might be just a little upset at having the corpse of my father standing—standing, mark you—in the very room in which I passed through puberty with such flying colours? Eh?
Marge Well, I don't see what that's got to do with it . . .
Weston I came to grips with all of nature's complexities in that room. Unravelled the riddles. And now this! What was the point of all that pain?
Marge Don't go in if it's going to upset you.
Weston I don't have to go in. It's the thought!
Marge You'll feel better when it's been explained properly.
Weston Who can possibly explain this?
Marge The man from the museum's coming round tomorrow.
Weston (*horrified*) She's not sticking you in the Evolution of Man section first, is she?

Marge Course not. He's from the taxidermal department. He'll explain how they go about it.
Weston I see. He'll be reassuring Butter, will he? Tell him it won't hurt a bit, that sort of thing?
Butter He's just going to explain.
Weston Have you told him exactly what he's going to have to explain?
Marge Not yet.
Weston Poor sod!
Marge It won't bother him. He'll have done it hundreds of times.

There is a pause

Weston (*to Butter*) Is this what you want?
Butter It's what your mother wants, Weston. It's not going to bother me one way or the other when it comes to it. Try to understand your mother. I know it's difficult just now, what with the shock and everything. But try to understand.
Weston I'm afraid my powers of understanding are at a rather low ebb just now. Having just found out that I've been raised by a ... a ghoul all these years ...
Marge Oh, it's no use, Dad, not while he's in this mood. We should have waited. We'll talk about it in the morning.
Weston No, we won't. I want to know now. I want to know why. Why do you want my father stuffed and put in a glass cabinet like someone else's antique crockery? What possible reason can you have?
Marge Company.
Weston Company?
Marge Someone to talk to still.
Weston Christ, Marge, you can't hold a conversation with a corpse. Or are you going to have a tape recorder installed in his back, so that every time you press his nose in, he says, "Hello, Marge, how about a nice cup of tea?"
Marge I don't expect him to talk back, of course I don't expect that. But I can still talk to him and imagine that he's talking to me. I can tell him all my problems and imagine he's giving me the answers.
Weston I'll get you a parrot.
Marge Oh, it's no use.
Weston Most widows are satisfied with a pet of some description.

Marge (*bitterly*) I know. Loving sons and daughters go out specially to the pet shop and buy them.
Weston That's right ...
Marge And then they go home and think, thank God she's got some company and we're not lumbered.
Butter Listen to what your mother's telling you, son.
Weston I'm listening but I'm not getting any sense. Why would anyone in their right mind want a stuffed corpse for company?
Marge (*fiercely*) Because I'm old! Because I'm frightened! Because I'll be so lonely!
Weston You've got me ...
Marge You? I haven't got you. Patricia's got you.
Weston You've got us. We'll visit ...
Marge Just like you've visited the last three months?
Weston We'll stay if you like. Or you can come and stay with us.
Marge That would never work. Living with your old mum? What kind of life would that be for a young fancy-piece like your Patricia?
Weston We'll work something out.
Marge And if I did come and stay, what then? I couldn't share anything with you.
Weston What are you talking about?
Marge I couldn't share anything with you because you're not old.
Weston Don't be soft, Marge.
Marge Soft, is it? Would you worry about coming home late of an evening? No, but I would. You wouldn't worry about the cold, or shopping, or the pension rate—or death. But I would. Because I'm old. I worry old people's worries. How could you understand that? It would be like a brick wall between us, like you weren't there at all. But you would be there and that would make it ten times worse. We'd be at each other's throats in a month.
Weston There are clubs you can go to, you can meet new friends, socialize with them.
Marge It's too late for that.
Weston You haven't tried.
Marge It's too late. I've spent fifty-five years of my life not wanting anyone else outside this room. How can I start now?
Weston You have to. You have to be with people, whatever age, not with a corpse.

Marge It'll be a comfort.
Weston There are other ways of finding comfort, love. Better ways.
Marge Like moving into a Home? That's the alternative, isn't it? That's the final solution. I'd be out of your hair then, wouldn't I? Except for Sundays, of course, when you'd feel obliged to visit. But even that would tail off eventually.
Weston My God, you are a selfish woman. My father is dying and all you can think about is what is going to happen to you.
Butter But that's all that matters now. I know where I'm going. It's Marge who has to face the future. Where's she going?
Marge I'm going into a Home, Dad, that's where I'm going ...
Weston Look, no-one is going to stick you in a bloody Home ...
Marge And when I go, I'm taking Butter with me.
Weston Oh, Jesus Christ, Marge ... (*Pause*) Look, don't you realize that having Butter upstairs in a cabinet is a short-cut to a Home? It's a short-cut to the bloody loony bin. They'll think you're a bloody loony and what's more, they'll be right. (*Pause*) It won't look like Butter, you know.
Marge What do you mean? It will be Butter.
Weston His skin, yes. But his soul won't be there and it's the soul that creates the personality that you love. Smile, Butter.
Butter What for?
Weston Just smile for a minute.

Butter grins broadly

There you are. That's personality, that lovely smile.

He strokes Butter's face

And those wrinkles, those friendly old wrinkles. They'll go. His face'll be all smooth and stretched and lifeless. They probably won't even use his own skin. No, it'll be some plastic imitation rubbish, something that'll keep. He'll be a fire hazard. (*Pause*) Come on, Marge. You've had a shock, you're apprehensive about the future. Well, who isn't? You're not alone in that, we've all got worries. I understand. And, together, we'll work something out for the future.

Marge I wouldn't mind living on my own. I won't be a bother to anyone if I had Butter still.
Weston We haven't forgotten you. I know we haven't been

around in the last few months, but we've just got married, bought a new house. We had to do it up, I told you that on the phone. There was a lot of work to be done.
Butter You see, Marge.
Weston We'll visit as often as you like. Count on it.
Marge You say that. I reckon it'll be different when Patricia has her say.
Weston (*exasperated*) What in God's name are you talking about now?
Marge I'm talking about what is going to happen, whether you can see it or not. I know you'll visit occasionally. Once a month, maybe. Birthdays, Christmas. But not much more. And I'll need more. That's why I want my Butter. I'll need him 'til the day I die. And if the man from the museum says he can do it, I'm having him done.
Weston Yes, well, I reckon I've got a say in this as well and I say, no way.
Butter It'll be in my will, son. There's nothing you can do.
Weston I'll contest.
Butter No, you wouldn't want to do that, would you? All that fuss? What does it matter?
Weston Plenty to me. I don't want my last memories of you to be a grotesque face—no offence, Butter—staring out at me from behind a sheet of glass. I want to remember the happy days. The walks, the picnics, the laughs . . .
Butter You don't have to go in. Simple as that. It's just for your mother.
Weston (*to Marge*) You just can't bear to let go, can you? You couldn't let go for a minute in fifty years and now the grip's just got so tight. Well, you're going to have to let go, because you can't stop death. That's what we're talking about, Marge. Death. Butter is dying and when he's dead, he'll be gone. There's nothing you can do. Do you know what? I'm glad. I'm glad he's getting away at last because you've possessed him too long. You've suffocated him, you've . . .

Marge in tears, slaps him hard and runs from the room

Oh God, Marge, I'm sorry . . . (*He starts to go after her*)
Butter It's all right. She needs to cry. Ever since I told her I had cancer, she's never cried.

Weston I'd better say something...
Butter Leave her. She needs it.

There is a pause

Butter clears up the tray on the table and takes it into the kitchen. He returns

Here, are you really glad I'm dying?
Weston Course I'm not, you silly bugger.
Butter That's what you said.
Weston It's not what I meant. I didn't mean any of that. (*Pause*) Are you glad?
Butter I can cope. Coping's the main thing.
Weston How do you cope? How can you take this so calmly?
Butter I've accepted it. I didn't have much choice. The doctors tried their best, but...
Weston And you? Did you try your best?
Butter Course I did.
Weston Took your pills, did what they told you?
Butter To the letter.
Weston Then why didn't they do any good?
Butter It was a bigger job than they thought. These things happen. You've got to help your mother now.
Weston She needs help, doesn't she?
Butter Yes she does.
Weston I'll get her the best, don't you worry about that. I know a couple of good psycho quacks. I'm owed a couple of favours in that line, as a matter of fact...
Butter That's not what she needs...
Weston God, what an evening. Father's dying, mother's going ga-ga...
Butter (*raising his voice for the first time*) Your mother is no different from anyone else in her position. She needs you, Weston, not a doctor. *You*, Weston.
Weston I need some fresh air. My head's buzzing.
Butter Go on. Go for a walk. It'll give you time to think.
Weston I'd rather stay with you.
Butter I'll still be here when you get back.
Weston Course you will. Plenty of time yet. Three months? What do they know? It could be a year yet. Three years, probably,

they've not got much right so far. And that's a long time. We've still got a long time.
Butter Plenty time.

There is a long pause

Weston I love you, Dad.
Butter And I love you, son.

Weston exits

Butter sighs deeply

Why can't he understand?

There is a pause

Trish enters

Trish Mind if I come in?
Butter By all means, Trish, come on in. Want the telly?
Trish (*shaking her head*) Rather talk.
Butter So would I.
Trish What's been happening through here? Marge is in tears.
Butter They had a bit of a barney, I'm afraid.
Trish I told him not to lose his temper. I told him.
Butter He's gone for a walk.
Trish I saw him go.
Butter He's taken it hard.
Trish Can you blame him?
Butter I suppose not. If he could see the funny side of it, it would be easier.
Trish You should have waited. Telling him you're going to die was bad enough, but ... It's hard to see the funny side right now.
Butter I have a good giggle about it myself. When Marge isn't here, of course. She takes it very seriously at the moment.
Trish I noticed. (*Pause*) It's funny.
Butter I'm glad you think so too.
Trish No, no I don't, not really. It's just funny that you're the only person who thinks it's funny.
Butter (*smiling*) Yes, now that is funny, isn't it? (*Pause*) Don't worry about Weston, love. He'll have a good laugh about it himself eventually.

Trish I'm not worried about Weston. I'm worried about Marge. It's like she doesn't accept that you're going to be gone. When the heart and lungs stop working, she's just going to replace them with something else and carry on as if nothing's happened.
Butter Once Marge comes to accept, she'll forget that she even thought about having me stuffed.
Trish Do you think she ever will accept?
Butter I think she has. You don't cry if everything's going to carry on as normal. (*Pause*) I was reading an article about you tonight. In Vo-gu.
Trish In what?
Butter The fashion magazine.
Trish (*smiling*) Oh ... yes.
Butter Says that you were a top-notch model once.
Trish I had my moments.
Butter Fancy Weston not saying.
Trish Well, I'd given it up by the time we got married.
Butter Is that why you gave it up?
Trish God no. Weston tried to persuade me to go back to it. To be honest, Butter—you don't mind me calling you that, do you?
Butter Everyone else does.
Trish Well, to be honest, we need the money.
Butter Weston said you were rolling in it.
Trish (*smiling*) Well, you know Weston ... (*Pause*) He's a good agent but he's not West End class just yet.

There is a pause

Butter I'm not being rude, Trish, you mustn't think I'm being rude, but, well, you don't look like your typical top-notch model, either.
Trish Ah yes, but there are models and then there are models. I'm afraid my assets are not the ones you would look for in your typical top-notch model.
Butter What are they?
Trish My hands. Apparently they could make green washing-up liquid look like sparkling champagne.
Butter Let's have a look.

Trish shows him her hands

You bite your nails!

Trish I didn't used to. I used to spend entire mornings manicuring them, entire days looking after my hands. God, what a waste.
Butter Giving it up?
Trish Doing it. The boredom, the endless hours of being fussed over by idiots. So I gave it up, went home and bit all ten fingers to the bone. Best meal I ever had.
Butter High protein diet. Very important.

They laugh. There is a pause

Anyway, (*he indicates Trish's bump*) you've more important things to think about now.
Trish It all seems so dreadfully ironic now.
Butter You mustn't think like that. It's like destiny. One born, one dies. Makes you believe in fate, doesn't it?
Trish No. I think it's horrible. (*Pause*) You want to die, don't you?
Butter What makes you say a thing like that?
Trish I've watched you. There's no fear. It's almost as if you're looking forward to some long holiday in the sun.
Butter I don't want to die, Trish. It's not been one of my life's ambitions.
Trish Then why this calm, this unnatural calm? (*Pause*)
Butter When they told me I had cancer, they gave me this long spiel about the treatment I was going to get. All the pills, the radium, the lot. And most important, they said, you've got to believe that you're going to beat it. Well, I went home that night and thought to myself, I'm not going to beat it, this is going to kill me. This is the finish. And Trish, you think I'm calm? I cried like a baby, like a little baby. I don't want to die. But that's like someone who likes the sun crying about nightfall. I mean, death, Trish, it's natural. Why should we be afraid? What makes me laugh is all the trouble we go to preserve life. It doesn't seem to matter what state we're in, as long as we look alive. That's the main thing. Every death fills us with horror, yet it happens to everyone. We battle against it like children trying to stop the tide knocking down their sandcastles on the beach. They shore them up with any old rubbish, but they know that the bad old sea is going to get them in the end. All the new fangled concoctions doctors come up with just to make us live a couple of years longer.

Trish You are allowed to live a couple of years longer, you know. It isn't against the law.
Butter (*gently*) My time has come. It's something you know instinctively. Like the animals know, only they don't have doctors to talk them out of it. I'm not going to battle against the inevitable. Like Weston said, what's the point of all that pain?
Trish Weston said that?
Butter He wasn't talking about death. He was talking about puberty at the time.
Trish There always was a Freudian streak about him.
Butter Yes. He mentioned him and all. (*Pause*) I've lived my life, I've enjoyed my life, I wouldn't have changed a minute of my life. (*Pause*) Not much to cry about in that statement, is there, Trish?
Trish Is that what you're going to tell Marge? That there isn't much to cry about?
Butter But she's got everything to cry about. She's the one left behind and she's scared.
Trish She won't be alone.
Butter I know.

Marge enters

Marge ...
Trish Are you feeling better?
Marge Yes, thank you. I don't know what came over me. Pleased at seeing Weston, I expect. (*Pause*) Well, I've made up Weston's room. I expect you're tired.
Trish Yes. (*Pause*) Can I make you anything ...?
Marge No. I'll have a cup of tea with Dad later on.

There is a pause

Trish All right. I ... goodnight. (*She kisses Butter*)
Butter Goodnight, Trish. Sleep well.
Marge Goodnight.

Trish exits

There is silence

That's another day then.
Butter Fresh one starts tomorrow.

Marge I don't care if it doesn't. It's not fair. (*She moves to Butter, tears welling up in her eyes*) It's just not fair. Oh Dad . . .

She lets out a cry of anguish as Butter holds her

Butter Ssh, Marge, ssh. It's all right. It's all right . . .

Fade to Black-out

CURTAIN

FURNITURE AND PROPERTY LIST

On stage: Seating for four people, including a settee
Coal fire
Bookcase. *On it:* telephone, notepad, pen and lamp *In it:* copy of Vogue
Coffee-table

Off stage: Tea tray set for four people, with scones and plates **(Marge)**
Bottle of champagne, glasses **(Trish)**

Personal: **Trish:** pregnancy padding

LIGHTING PLOT

Practical fittings required: table lamp

Interior. The same scene throughout

To open: *gradually fading daylight*

Cue 1	**Butter** closes the curtains and switches on a lamp *Snap on practical, increase lighting overall*	(Page 8)
Cue 2	**Butter**: "It's all right. It's all right ..." *Fade to black-out*	(Page 29)

EFFECTS PLOT

Cue 1	**Marge:** "I love you." *Sound of a car horn*	(Page 7)
Cue 2	**Marge:** "Look at my hands, they're shaking." *The doorbell rings frantically*	(Page 7)

MADE AND PRINTED IN GREAT BRITAIN BY
LATIMER TREND & COMPANY LTD PLYMOUTH
MADE IN ENGLAND

www.ingramcontent.com/pod-product-compliance
Lightning Source LLC
Chambersburg PA
CBHW070454050426
42450CB00012B/3269